How to Revise
for 11+

To do your best in the 11+ tests, it helps to be *totally* prepared. That's why
the experts at CGP have lovingly made this incredible all-in-one guide...

It's packed with advice on what to expect and the best ways to study — plus handy
Topic Planners to track your work. Nobody explains the 11+ better than CGP!

The Complete Guide

Contents

Published by CGP

Editors:
Sammy El-Bahrawy, Zoe Fenwick, Katie Fernandez, Emily Forsberg, Alison Palin, Gabrielle Richardson, Caley Simpson
With thanks to Sharon Keeley-Holden, Holly Robinson and Sean Walsh for the proofreading.
With thanks to Jan Greenway for the copyright research.

Please note that CGP is not associated with CEM in any way.
This book does not include any official questions and is not endorsed by CEM.

ISBN: 978 1 78908 408 5   Printed by Elanders Ltd, Newcastle upon Tyne.
Clipart from Corel®
Based on the classic CGP style created by Richard Parsons.

Text, design, layout and original illustrations © Coordination Group Publications Ltd. (CGP) 2019
All rights reserved.

How To Use This Book

There's lots to think about for the 11+, but this guide will point you in the right direction.

Advice is Organised into Clear Sections

The book is split into sections that are packed with <u>advice</u> and <u>techniques</u> to set you on the right path to <u>11+ success</u>.

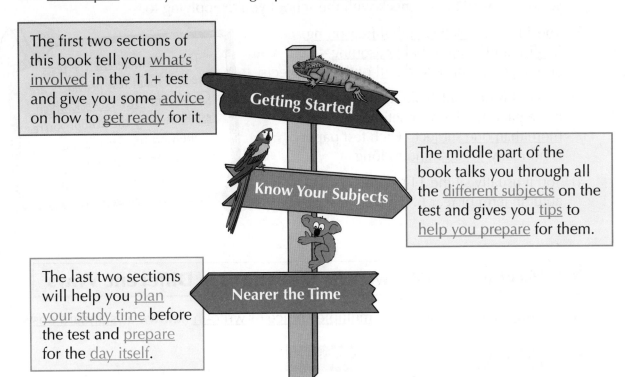

The first two sections of this book tell you <u>what's involved</u> in the 11+ test and give you some <u>advice</u> on how to <u>get ready</u> for it.

Getting Started

Know Your Subjects

The middle part of the book talks you through all the <u>different subjects</u> on the test and gives you <u>tips</u> to <u>help you prepare</u> for them.

The last two sections will help you <u>plan your study time</u> before the test and <u>prepare</u> for the <u>day itself</u>.

Nearer the Time

Plan Your Preparation in the Last Section

1) The last section of the book contains <u>Topic Planners</u> and a <u>Study Diary</u> for you to fill in.

2) Topic Planners are a good place to <u>list</u> everything you need to <u>be able to do</u> for the test.

3) A Study Diary is a great way to <u>record</u> the work you've done and see <u>what you've got left</u> to do.

4) Once you've read the book and filled in your Topic Planners, it's time to <u>get stuck in</u>...

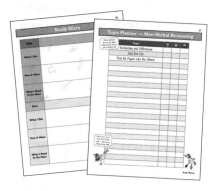

About the 11+

The 11+ is a test some secondary schools use to help them decide which students to accept. They may also look at things like where you live.

The 11+ Covers Up To **Four Different Subjects**

1) How the 11+ is tested <u>varies</u> from place to place. To find out <u>exactly</u> what you need to do, check with the <u>school</u> you're applying to.

2) The 11+ tests <u>Maths</u>, <u>Verbal Reasoning</u>, <u>English</u> and <u>Non-Verbal Reasoning</u> — but you might not have to do <u>all</u> of these subjects.

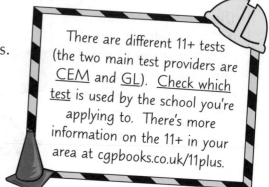

There are different 11+ tests (the two main test providers are <u>CEM</u> and <u>GL</u>). <u>Check which test</u> is used by the school you're applying to. There's more information on the 11+ in your area at cgpbooks.co.uk/11plus.

3) The test is normally split into <u>two or more</u> papers, which sometimes cover <u>more than one subject</u>. Each test paper is normally <u>45-60 minutes</u> long.

4) You'll usually sit the 11+ in the <u>autumn term of Year 6</u>.

You Might Have to Answer the **Questions** in **Different Ways**

The <u>questions</u> in the test can be <u>multiple choice</u> or <u>write-in</u> (known as <u>standard answer</u>).

Multiple Choice

- These give you <u>four or five answer options</u> to choose from.
- You <u>might</u> need to fill in your answers on a <u>separate sheet of paper</u>.

Write-In

- You may have to <u>write some answers yourself</u>.
- Questions can ask you to <u>fill in the blanks</u> — e.g. to complete a word.
- You might have to give your answer in <u>full sentences</u> (for example, on some <u>English</u> tests).

Make sure you know what to expect from the 11+...

You might have already done some tests at school, but the 11+ test will probably be quite different. Don't panic if it seems a bit scary at first — the tips in this book will help you prepare.

Organisation and Planning

Planning your work properly and being organised can make your preparation for the 11+ go really smoothly — it will save you time and help you keep track of your progress.

Plan Your Time...

✓ Start well before the test — that way, you'll have plenty of time to cover everything and lots of time left for things you enjoy too.

✓ Keep track of your progress using the Topic Planners and Study Diary at the back of this book.

✓ Prioritise topics you find tricky — don't put them off. Give yourself plenty of time to get to grips with them.

✓ Make sure you take plenty of breaks — a break from studying gives your brain time to process what it's learning.

> Try to fill your breaks with things you enjoy doing, like playing sport or spending time with friends.

... and Make Sure You Have Everything You Need

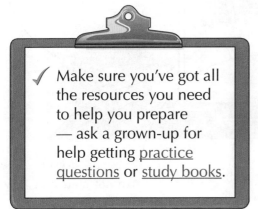

✓ Make sure you've got all the resources you need to help you prepare — ask a grown-up for help getting practice questions or study books.

✓ You'll need lots of paper, a pencil, a pencil sharpener and a rubber.

Plan your work and work your plan...

Preparing for the 11+ doesn't have to take over your life. If you're organised, and have a clear idea of what you're going to practise and when, you'll find plenty of time for work AND fun.

Your Study Space

When you're preparing for the 11+, it's important to stay focused. A good place to study is key — you're unlikely to work well if you're surrounded by distractions.

Think About Where You're Going to Work

1) You're probably going to be doing most of your 11+ preparation at home, so it's important to get into good study habits.

2) It's a good idea to work in the same place all the time if you can — this will make it easier to separate relaxation time and work time when you're at home.

3) A clutter-free study space is important — have a look at this one:

You could close the door to shut out any noise.

A well-lit space makes it easy to read.

No distractions — if you have a phone, laptop or tablet, turn them off. Make sure the TV is turned off too.

Make sure your table is tidy and your stationery is nearby.

Choose a table with enough space to work.

A panda, because — well, I'm not quite sure how he got there actually...

A tidy space is important, but don't spend hours setting it up...

Instead of working, it's tempting to spend a long time making your study space perfectly neat and tidy. Your time is much better spent actually doing the work though.

Looking After Yourself

Studying for the test is important, but make sure you're looking after yourself properly too.

Take Care of Yourself Before the Test

If you're <u>well rested</u>, <u>relaxed</u> and you've <u>eaten</u> the <u>right things</u>, you'll find it easier to <u>learn</u> and <u>remember information</u>.

1) Get **Regular Exercise** and **Fresh Air**.
   Exercise is good for your brain <u>and</u> your body.

2) Try to Eat Lots of **Fruit and Veg**.
   Help your parents or carers pick it out at the supermarket so you get the fruit and veg you actually like.

3) Drink Plenty of <u>Water</u>.
   It'll help you stay focused.

4) Plan **Fun Things** to **Look Forward To**.
   Take regular breaks and fill them with things you enjoy doing.

5) Do Something <u>Relaxing</u> Before you go to <u>Bed</u>.
   You could read a book or listen to some music.

6) If you have a <u>Phone</u>, <u>Keep it Away</u> from your Bed.
   Looking at a screen makes it harder for your brain to switch off.

7) Get Enough **Sleep**.
   If you're tired, you won't learn or remember things properly.

Planning and Preparation Advice

Making a plan and following it should mean you feel prepared when test day arrives.

Make a Plan

Here's an example of how you could <u>plan</u> your practice for 11+ Maths:

You should make a plan for each subject you'll be tested on.

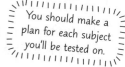

How long you spend on each step of your plan will depend on how much time you have before the test.

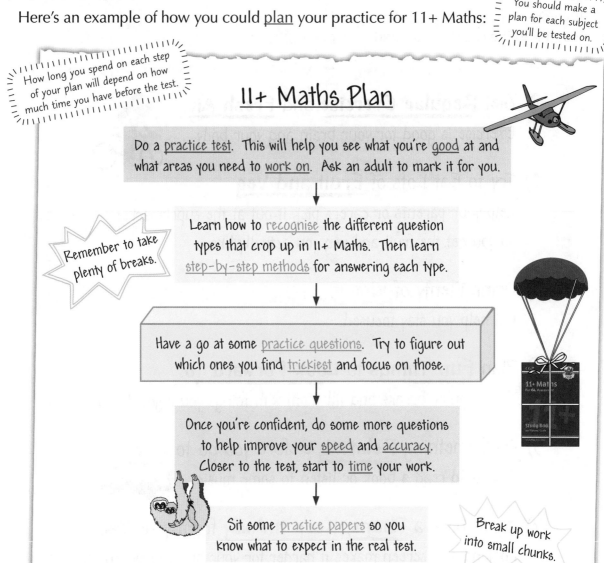

11+ Maths Plan

Do a <u>practice test</u>. This will help you see what you're <u>good</u> at and what areas you need to <u>work on</u>. Ask an adult to mark it for you.

Learn how to <u>recognise</u> the different question types that crop up in 11+ Maths. Then learn <u>step-by-step methods</u> for answering each type.

Remember to take plenty of breaks.

Have a go at some <u>practice questions</u>. Try to figure out which ones you find <u>trickiest</u> and focus on those.

Once you're confident, do some more questions to help improve your <u>speed</u> and <u>accuracy</u>. Closer to the test, start to <u>time</u> your work.

Sit some <u>practice papers</u> so you know what to expect in the real test.

Break up work into small chunks.

A good plan only works if you stick to it...

Don't panic if you didn't do very well on your first go — you'll have plenty of time to improve. Keep a record of your scores — this will let you track your progress and see what you're good at.

Getting Test Ready

The 11+ is a timed test, so you need to practise answering questions accurately and at speed.

Start by **Working** on **Accuracy**...

1) When you start practising, make sure you know <u>what you have to do</u> and that you're getting the questions <u>right</u>. Don't worry about speed yet.

2) Try some <u>practice questions</u> and ask an adult to mark them for you. Then <u>go over</u> the questions you got <u>wrong</u>. You can look at the <u>answers</u> and see how you should have solved them.

3) If there's a particular topic or question type you often get <u>wrong</u>, <u>practise</u> lots of these questions until you're <u>confident</u> with them.

... then **Work** on **Speed**

In the real 11+ test, you'll have a <u>set amount</u> of time to answer all of the questions. The <u>faster</u> you are, the <u>more</u> questions you'll be able to answer.

Here are some <u>tips</u> to help you <u>improve your speed</u>:

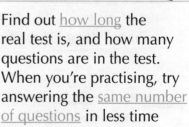

Answer 20 questions as <u>quickly</u> as you can (time yourself with a stopwatch). Now try another set of 20 questions — see if you can answer them in <u>less time</u> than your first go.

<u>Only check</u> your answers <u>if you</u> have time at the end of the test.

Find out <u>how long</u> the real test is, and how many questions are in the test. When you're practising, try answering the <u>same number of questions</u> in less time than you'll actually have.

Turn practising into a <u>game</u> — ask an adult to time each question with a <u>stopwatch</u> and then you can <u>ring a bell</u> or <u>make a funny noise</u> when you've solved it. Aim to get faster each time.

You can find out how long the test is by checking with the school you're applying for.

Ask an adult to <u>race</u> you when answering a set of 15 questions. See who can answer the questions the <u>quickest</u>.

Getting Test Ready

As **Test Day** gets **Closer**, Start **Working** on **Test Technique**

Try these things when working through <u>practice papers</u>
to help you develop a good <u>test technique</u>:

- Practise filling in <u>your details</u> on the front of <u>practice papers</u>.

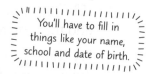
You'll have to fill in things like your name, school and date of birth.

- Don't be afraid to <u>skip questions</u>, but remember to <u>go back</u> to them at the <u>end</u>.

- If you're still <u>stuck</u> on something when you go back to it, <u>don't</u> leave it <u>blank</u> — making a <u>sensible guess</u> might get you the mark!

The best way to see what the <u>real test</u> might be like is to try some practice test papers under <u>test conditions</u> (see next page).

Practise Filling Out **Answer Sheets**

You might have to write your answers on a separate sheet.

If your test is in <u>multiple-choice format</u>, you need to fill in your answers in a particular way:

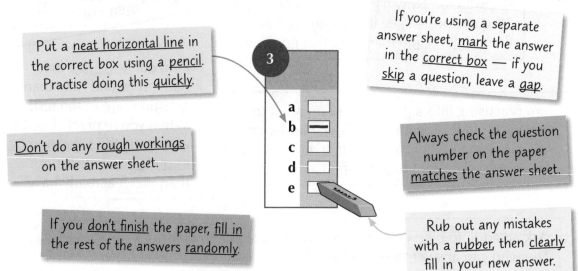

Put a <u>neat horizontal line</u> in the correct box using a <u>pencil</u>. Practise doing this <u>quickly</u>.

If you're using a separate answer sheet, <u>mark</u> the answer in the <u>correct box</u> — if you <u>skip</u> a question, leave a <u>gap</u>.

<u>Don't</u> do any <u>rough workings</u> on the answer sheet.

Always check the question number on the paper <u>matches</u> the answer sheet.

If you <u>don't finish</u> the paper, <u>fill in</u> the rest of the answers <u>randomly</u>.

Rub out any mistakes with a <u>rubber</u>, then <u>clearly</u> fill in your new answer.

Using Practice Papers

Doing practice papers under test conditions is as close as you'll get to the real thing.

Do as Many **Practice Papers** as You Can

The key to success in the 11+ is to be <u>well prepared</u> for the test.
To do this, you need to know what 11+ tests <u>look like</u>.

CGP's Practice Paper **Top Tips**

 ① <u>Practise under test conditions</u> sssh
- Make sure you have a <u>pencil</u>, a <u>rubber</u> and a <u>pencil sharpener</u>.
- Make sure you can see a <u>clock</u> or a <u>watch</u> and <u>time yourself</u> — don't use more time than you're allowed.
- Find somewhere quiet, with <u>no distractions</u> (see page 4).
- <u>Practise</u> doing papers <u>back-to-back</u> so you get used to <u>concentrating</u> for a long time <u>without breaks</u>.
- Before you begin, listen to an <u>online audio</u> recording of the <u>instructions</u> on the front of the practice paper, or ask an adult to <u>read</u> them out to you.

> Practise filling out your <u>information</u> on the front of your answer sheets.

 ② <u>If you have time at the end...</u>
- Go back to any questions you <u>missed out</u>.
- <u>Check over</u> your answers and correct any <u>mistakes</u>.
- Don't worry if you don't have time to check your answers though. It's more important to try to answer <u>all</u> the questions.

> Try doing the practice papers at the same time of day as the real test — they'll probably be first thing in the morning.

 ③ <u>Use the mark scheme</u> ✓
- Practice papers should have a <u>mark scheme</u>.
- These tell you the <u>correct answer</u> and how to get the right answer.
- Ask an adult to <u>mark your test</u> and help you see what you did wrong.

 ④ <u>Don't panic</u> !!!!
- If you don't get a high mark at first, <u>don't worry</u> — aim to get <u>a bit better each time</u>.
- If you ran out of time and didn't finish a test, work on <u>improving your speed</u> (see page 7).

The Perfect Hot Chocolate

A key part of your 11+ preparation is learning how to make the Perfect Hot Chocolate. It might even be the most important bit. (Okay, it's not, but it's certainly a delicious part...)

The **Ingredients**

Hot chocolate <u>powder</u>
<u>Milk</u>
<u>Hot water</u>
Mini <u>marshmallows</u>
Squirty <u>cream</u>
<u>Chocolate</u> flakes

Yummy cream

Choccy flakes

Creamy hot choc

Delicious goo layer

The **Equipment**

Your favourite <u>mug</u>
A <u>kettle</u>
A <u>teaspoon</u>

My favourite mug — just the right size (huge)

Oh no, they fell, I'll just have to eat them...

The **Method**

1) Put a <u>few scoops</u> of hot chocolate <u>powder</u> into your favourite mug (<u>check</u> how much you need on the <u>packet</u>). Add a small amount of <u>milk</u> and mix into a delicious chocolatey <u>paste</u>.

Trust me — it'll make your hot chocolate <u>nice and frothy</u>.

You can use milk instead of hot water for extra creaminess — heat the milk on the hob or in a microwave (ask a grown-up for help with this).

2) Ask a <u>grown-up</u> to put the <u>kettle on</u>. Let it <u>boil</u> and then <u>leave</u> it for a few minutes to <u>cool down</u>.

3) <u>Half-fill</u> your mug with hot water, then give it a <u>good stir</u> (bye bye nasty powder lumps). <u>Top up</u> with more hot water until it's almost full and <u>stir again</u>.

4) Add a <u>layer of marshmallows</u>, then lots of <u>cream</u>. Top with more <u>marshmallows</u> and <u>chocolate flakes</u>.

The marshmallows form a <u>melty goo barrier</u> to stop the cream melting too quickly.

5) <u>Sit back</u>, <u>relax</u> and <u>enjoy</u> your Perfect Hot Chocolate ☺

How To ~~Prepare~~ make the perfect hot chocolate

Know Your Subjects

Now this is where the fun starts. You might have come across some of this stuff at school, but there are some things you won't have seen before.

There are **Four Main Subjects** to Learn

In the 11+, the four main subjects you could be tested on are:

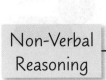

Non-Verbal Reasoning

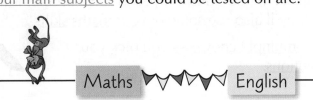

Maths   English

Verbal Reasoning

The questions asked in each subject can be divided into topics. For example, the topics in the Non-Verbal Reasoning part of the test can include:

Make sure you know if you'll be taking the CEM or GL test. There are differences in the subjects, topics and question types in each test. Check exactly what you need to know for your test — ask an adult to help you if you're not sure.

For example, English is only covered in GL, but some GL English topics are similar to ones in CEM Verbal Reasoning.

Non-Verbal Reasoning
- Similarities and Differences
- Pairs, Series and Grids
- Rotation and Reflection
- 3D Shapes and Folding
- Codes
- Spatial Reasoning

In This **Section...**

1) This section of the book goes through each topic in each subject, giving you examples of some types of question you might be asked.

2) There are some tips on how to tackle these question types, and things to think about when answering them.

3) You can also have a go at some questions yourself.

The pages will tell you if questions only come up in the CEM or GL test — you can ignore any topics or question types that won't be on your test.

Non-Verbal Reasoning

You probably won't have come across Non-Verbal Reasoning questions before.
But don't worry — these pages will tell you what they're all about.

Non-Verbal Reasoning is All About **Shapes** and **Diagrams**

Non-Verbal Reasoning (NVR) questions ask you to solve problems involving
shapes and patterns. They'll also use some of your maths skills.

All of the questions are multiple choice — you pick your
answer from a set of options.

There are Some **Key Things** You'll Want to Look Out For

There are a few things that come up a lot in Non-Verbal Reasoning questions.
You should look out for these in each question.

Shapes
You need to pay attention to what shapes there are,
how many sides they have, and things like symmetry.

Rotation and Reflection
Shapes can be turned around or flipped.

Position Position Position
Shapes can be in different positions — bottom,
middle or top, left or right, front or back.

Order
The order of shapes in a figure
might change or move around.

Shading and lines
Shapes can be filled in or blank, or shaded
in different ways (spotted, lines, grey or
black). Lines can be solid, dotted or dashed.

Layering
Overlapping shapes may
change position, layer or colour.

Pointing
Arrows can point in a particular
direction, or they can be pointing
towards or away from something.

Counting
Be prepared to count things like numbers
of different shapes, or features of the
shape (such as the number of sides).

Non-Verbal Reasoning

Whichever 11+ test you're taking, you'll need to be able to look for similarities and differences between figures to spot the one that is most like or most unlike the others.

Similarities and Differences Questions

Examples

There could be 4, 5 or 6 options to choose from, depending on which test you're taking.

1) Find the figure which is most unlike the others.

a   b   c   (d)   e

The answer is **d**. In all the other figures, the outline of the shape is dashed.

2) Work out which option is most like the two figures on the left.

  |

a   (b)   c   d   e

The answer is **b**. In the figures on the left, the shapes in the middle column are white. There is one grey, one black and one white shape in each of the left and right columns.

When answering these questions, you should:

- Check carefully whether you need to find the figure most like or unlike the rest.
- Take your time to go through the options. Some features are there to distract you from the real pattern, so be careful not to rush and get caught out.

Here's a question to try for yourself. The answer is on page 63.

Work out which option is most like the three figures on the left.

    |

a   b   c   d   e

Non-Verbal Reasoning

Some CEM and GL questions might ask you to find the figure that completes a set.

Pairs, Series and Grids

You might need to work out what <u>fills the gap</u> in a <u>pair</u>, <u>series</u> or <u>grid</u> of figures.

Examples

1) The first figure is changed in some way to become the second. Choose the figure on the right that relates to the third figure like the second does to the first.

                        a   **b**   **ⓒ**   **d**   **e**

The answer is **c**. The shape is cut along the dashed line.
The lower part becomes grey. The upper part is reflected vertically.

2) On the left is a big square with one small empty square. Find which of the five squares on the right should replace the empty square.

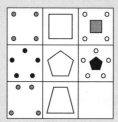

                       a   **b**   **c**   **d**   **ⓔ**

The answer is **e**. Working from left to right, the third grid square is made
up of the dots in the first grid square and a smaller version of the shape
in the second grid square. The shape and the dots swap shading.

Complete the Pair

In the GL test, there is only <u>one pair</u> of figures that have changed on the left. In the CEM test, there could be <u>two pairs</u>.

Complete the Series

In the GL test, there is a <u>set of five</u> figures in order with one missing. In the CEM test, the set may contain a different number of figures.

Complete the Grid

In the GL test, the grid can be made up of either <u>four or nine squares</u>. In the CEM test, the grid could be made up of either <u>squares or hexagons</u>.

Non-Verbal Reasoning

CEM asks specific questions on rotation and reflection. However, you need to be able to spot rotations and reflections for GL as well — they might come up within other questions.

Rotation and Reflection

You might need to work out how a figure will look if it is <u>rotated</u> or <u>reflected</u>. There'll be an <u>arrow</u> or a <u>line</u> given in the question to show <u>which</u> rotation or reflection to do.

Examples

1) Which option would look like the figure on the left if it was rotated?

a   b   c   d

The answer is **a**. The figure is rotated 90 degrees anticlockwise.
Option **b** is a rotated reflection. In option **c**, the triangle is pointing in the wrong direction. In option **d**, the triangle is in the wrong position.

A rotation of 90 degrees anticlockwise is the same as a rotation of 270 degrees clockwise.

2) Which option would look like the figure on the left if it was reflected over the line?

Reflect   a   b   c   d

The answer is **b**. In option **a**, the grey and white shapes have swapped shading.
Option **c** is a 180 degree rotation. Option **d** is a reflection across a vertical line.

Here are some helpful things to do when answering rotation and reflection questions:

- Find a <u>distinctive part</u> of the figure, then <u>rule out</u> any options which don't have this feature. Repeat this with other features.

- For reflection questions, first look at the <u>biggest shape</u> in the figure. Imagine what its <u>reflection</u> will look like and <u>rule out</u> any options which don't match this. Then move onto other parts of the figure and do the same.

- For rotation questions, try <u>turning your book</u> or practice paper round to see what each figure looks like the right way up.

Non-Verbal Reasoning

These questions could come up on both tests (they're part of 'spatial reasoning' for GL).

3D Shapes and Folding

Question types can include <u>rotating</u> and <u>combining shapes</u> in <u>3D space</u>, and imagining the <u>top-down 2D view</u> of a <u>3D figure</u>. You might also need to imagine what a <u>2D net</u> looks like when it's folded into a <u>3D shape</u>, and what a 2D shape looks like when it's <u>folded</u> or <u>unfolded</u>.

Examples

1) Which set of blocks can be put together to make the 3D figure on the left?

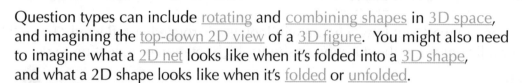

The answer is **b**. The bottom block in **b** is to the left of the figure, with the other two blocks arranged to the right of it.

2) Which option shows the figure on the left when folded along the dotted line?

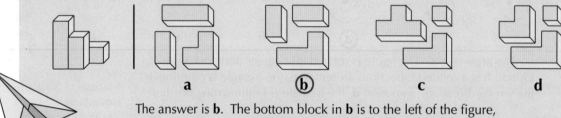

The answer is **b**. It can't be **a** or **d** because the part of the figure originally to the right of the fold line is the wrong shape. Option **c** is ruled out because the part of the figure originally to the left of the fold line is the wrong shape. Option **e** is ruled out because the fold line has moved.

Here's another question for you to try. You'll find the answer on page 63.

Work out which of the five cubes can be made from the net.

Q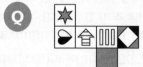

a   b   c   d   e

Non-Verbal Reasoning

This page covers some question types you might come across in the GL test.

Codes

In these questions, you'll need to work out what <u>feature</u> each <u>code letter</u> stands for. You then need to use these to <u>work out the code</u> for another figure.

You can get questions where the figures on the left are laid out vertically as well.

Example

On the left are some figures with code letters. Work out what the code letters mean and decide which of the codes on the right goes with the new figure.

a   b   ⓒ   d   e

The answer is **c** (DU).
B = five-pointed white star,   C = four-pointed white star,   D = six-pointed white star.
U = bottom star is grey,   V = bottom star is black.

A good starting point is to look for code letters which appear <u>more than once</u> and see what <u>similarities</u> these figures have. It also helps to <u>write down</u> what each letter means as you work it out.

Spatial Reasoning

Some GL tests also include spatial reasoning questions — some will be similar to the <u>3D Shapes and Folding</u> questions on the previous page, but there are other question types too. Here's an example of a <u>Hidden Shape</u> question:

Example

You might also be given some shapes and asked how they will look when they're joined together in a certain way.

In which figure is the shape on the left hidden?

a   b   ⓒ   d   e   The answer is **c**.

Fun Ways to Prepare for NVR

If you want a break from the more serious side of practice, here are some bits and bobs you can try that might help you flex your spatial awareness and Non-Verbal Reasoning skills.

There are **Fun Ways** to Help **Develop** Your **Skills**

It's time to get arty-crafty. For these activities, you're going to need: building blocks or modelling clay, scissors, paper, pencils, crayons, glue and a hole punch.

Model Making

A lot of people find it tricky to imagine what 3D shapes will look like when viewed from a different angle or after a rotation. To help with this, try making some different 3D shapes out of blocks or modelling clay, then rotate them and sketch how they look. And if your 3D model happens to be a fort or a pirate ship, even better!

Nets

You might have made nets for cubes in school. Try making nets with different designs on each face. Predict which sides will meet each other when the net is folded up. Then make the cube from the net and see if your predictions were correct. This is a good way to practise your spatial reasoning skills.

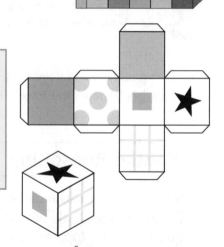

Spot the Difference

Spot the Difference is a big deal in Non-Verbal Reasoning — so why not have a go at some? There are lots of puzzle books which have Spot the Difference puzzles in them.

Another way to help you pay close attention to detail is using books where you have to find something in a big complicated picture, such as the 'Where's Wally?' books.

Fun Ways to Prepare for NVR

Hole Punch

Fold up a square piece of paper and use a hole punch to make a hole through it. Try guessing what the paper will look like before you unfold it. Then unfold the piece of paper to see where the holes are. This will help develop your skills for the paper folding questions.

Snowflakes and Paper Dolls

Making snowflakes, paper doll chains and similar paper shapes are a fun way to spend a rainy afternoon. If your parents or carers get grumpy about all the little bits of paper that end up on the floor, just tell them it's for the 11+.

PAPER SNOWFLAKES

1. Take a square piece of paper.
2. Fold the square in half diagonally and then fold it in half two more times.
3. Cut the 'top' of the triangle off so it looks like this:
4. Carefully cut out different shapes from the edges (make sure some of the folded edges stay intact).
5. Unfold the paper to see your snowflake.
6. Make more snowflakes! See how cutting the paper in different places affects the end result.

PAPER DOLLS

1. Take a piece of A4 paper and cut it in half lengthways.
2. Fold the paper into quarters, using a zig-zag fold:
3. Draw the outline of a symmetrical person on the top layer. Make sure the arms touch both edges of the paper.
4. Cut out the person through all the layers of the paper and then unfold the paper.
5. You should now have a chain of four symmetrical dolls.
6. Colour in the dolls however you want!
7. Make another chain. See what effect drawing a non-symmetrical person has on the end result.

Oops!

The fun doesn't end there...

Doing jigsaws, tangrams and 3D logic puzzles (where you have to fit together a number of different pieces to make a new shape) will help develop your problem-solving and spatial awareness skills. You can also play games like Snap to practise spotting similarities at speed.

Maths

Whether you love it or hate it, you'll have to tackle some Maths in the 11+ test as well.

Maths Questions can Cover Anything from School

You'll be happy to hear that you'll have already learned <u>most</u> of the Maths topics on the 11+ <u>at school</u>. However, the questions might be <u>harder</u> than what you've seen before.

There might also be <u>some bits</u> that you <u>haven't</u> learned about <u>yet</u>.
Look at the topics below to see if there's anything you <u>still need to learn</u>.

Number and Calculation

- Place value, ordering, negative numbers
- +, −, ×, ÷ and BODMAS
- Rounding and estimating $\quad 7\overline{)1\,^19\,^59\,^21}$ **2 7 3**
- Square and cube numbers
- Primes, multiples and factors

Ratio and Proportion

- Ratio problems
- Proportion
- Enlarging shapes using scale factors

Recipe for 1 cake
- 2 eggs
- 125 g flour

Fractions, Decimals and Percentages

- Converting between them
- Comparing and ordering them
- Equivalent fractions
- +, −, × and ÷ $\frac{2}{3}+\frac{1}{5}=\frac{10}{15}+\frac{3}{15}=\frac{13}{15}$

Algebra

- Writing and using formulas
- Sequences
- Finding missing numbers $3L + 2W = 9$ $L = 1, W = ?$

Measurement

- Length, mass, volume, time and money
- Converting units
- Perimeter, area and volume of shapes

Geometry

- 2D shapes (triangles, quadrilaterals, polygons and circles)
- 3D shapes and nets
- Angles and angle rules   54°

Position and Direction

- Coordinates
- Translation
- Reflection

Statistics

- Data and tables
- Charts and graphs
- Calculating the mean

Chart

Maths

CEM and GL both ask the same types of Maths questions in the 11+ tests.
You might see them as write-in or multiple-choice questions.

Working with Numbers

These are questions involving adding, subtracting, multiplying and dividing.
You might need to use place value, rounding or estimating in these questions too.

Example

Ade spends £5.20 on drinks from the menu shown.
Which of the options below shows the items he buys?

A One tea, one fruit smoothie

B Two teas, one hot chocolate

C Two hot chocolates

(D) One coffee, one hot chocolate

E Two coffees

Drinks Menu	
Tea	£1.50
Coffee	£2.45
Hot chocolate	£2.75
Fruit smoothie	£2.99

Add up the different options using
partitioning or by adding in columns.
The answer is **D**: £2.45 + £2.75 = £5.20.

Here's one for you to try.
The answer is on page 63.

27 × 128 = 3456

Q **What is 54 × 128?**

With multiple-choice questions, you
might be able to easily rule out
some options — e.g. in option A,
you can see that £1.50 + £2.99
will end in a 9, so it definitely won't
be the correct answer.

Number Knowledge

These are about different types of number, such as odd, even, square, cube and prime
numbers. They could also cover ratio, proportion, fractions, decimals and percentages.

Example

Ayla runs a rehoming centre for cats and dogs.
There are currently 56 animals at the centre.
For every 3 dogs, there are 4 cats.

How many cats are there at the centre?

This question is testing proportion.
Out of every 7 animals, 4 are cats.
56 animals is 8 lots of 7 animals,
so there are 8 × 4 = **32** cats.

Maths

Number **Problems**

These questions can involve spotting <u>number patterns</u> and continuing <u>sequences</u>.
You could also get <u>wordy questions</u>, where you'll have to <u>pick out</u> the <u>important details</u> —
note down the <u>key information</u>, then <u>decide</u> what maths you need to do to get the <u>answer</u>.

Example

Gita completed 3 challenges to raise money for charity. She was sponsored £65 for her run, twice as much for her swim, and £9 per mile for her bike ride. She raised £375 in total. How far was her bike ride?

Use the information to work out how much she was sponsored for her bike ride:
$£375 − £65 − (2 × £65) = £375 − £65 − £130 = £180$
Now divide this by the amount per mile: $£180 ÷ £9 = $ **20 miles**

Remember, you can check your calculations by doing the inverse. Here, you can multiply £9 by 20 to check that you get £180.

Data Handling

If a question includes a <u>table</u> or a <u>graph</u>, you might have to <u>read information</u> from it,
or fill in <u>missing numbers</u>. You might also have to calculate the <u>mean</u> of some data.

Example

Some pupils were asked which of dance, judo and drama they would prefer to do as an after-school club. The incomplete table below shows the results.

How many Year 5 pupils chose judo?

Look for where you can start filling in the gaps.
You can work out the number for Year 5 drama:
$19 − 8 − 8 = 3$
And the total for Year 5:
$74 − 25 − 27 = 22$
Now you've got all the Year 5 numbers, you need
to find the value for Year 5 judo: $22 − 9 − 3 = $ **10**

	Year 4	Year 5	Year 6	Total
Dance	12	9		
Judo	5			
Drama	8	3	8	19
Total	25	22	27	74

Drawing a table is easy — start with the top, then add some legs...

In some trickier maths questions, there might be more than one way to get the answer.
See if you can spot if there's an easier method you could use before diving straight in.

Maths

Shape and Space

There are <u>lots</u> of different types of questions you could get about <u>2D</u> and <u>3D shapes</u>.
Some of these involve <u>calculating</u> — e.g. <u>angles</u>, <u>area</u>, <u>perimeter</u> and <u>volume</u>.
Others might ask you to <u>reflect</u>, <u>rotate</u> or <u>translate</u> (shift) a shape.

Example

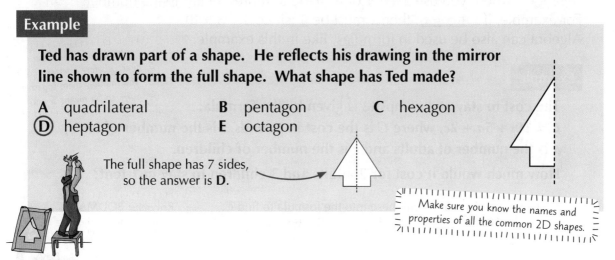

**Ted has drawn part of a shape. He reflects his drawing in the mirror
line shown to form the full shape. What shape has Ted made?**

A quadrilateral   **B** pentagon   **C** hexagon
D heptagon   **E** octagon

The full shape has 7 sides,
so the answer is **D**.

Make sure you know the names and
properties of all the common 2D shapes.

Units and Measures

You might need to use, calculate with, and <u>convert</u> between different <u>units</u> of
<u>measurement</u>. Common questions include units of: <u>length</u> (mm, cm, m, km),
<u>mass</u> (g, kg), <u>volume</u> (ml, litres), <u>time</u> (hours, mins, secs) and <u>money</u> (£, p).

Example

**Ashley makes 2.75 litres of soup. She fills six 400 ml containers with the soup,
and eats the rest for lunch. How much soup does Ashley eat for lunch?**

A 350 litres   **B** 750 ml   **C** 350 ml   **D** 0.35 ml   **E** 0.25 litres

Find the amount Ashley puts into containers: 6×400 ml = 2400 ml
The question uses both litres and ml, so make
them the same by converting 2.75 litres into ml: $2.75 \times 1000 = 2750$ ml
So Ashley eats 2750 – 2400 = 350 ml of soup — the answer is **C**.

Check that your answer
is sensible — answers
A and D wouldn't be
realistic amounts of
soup for one meal.

In questions with a <u>mix</u> of units, make sure you <u>convert</u> so that all of your numbers
are in the <u>same units</u>. The answer options might give you a <u>clue</u> about which unit
to choose, but if not, pick the one that makes the <u>maths easier</u>.

Maths

Unfortunately, there might be some questions on things you haven't seen before. Here are some of the common types of questions that often catch people out.

Algebra Problems

Algebra is where you use a <u>letter</u> or a <u>shape</u> to represent a <u>missing number</u>. For example, if <u>$x + 5 = 8$</u>, then x must be <u>3</u> (since $3 + 5 = 8$). Algebra can also be used in <u>formulas</u>, like in this example.

In algebra, a number directly before a letter means you multiply them together — so 5a means 5 × a.

Example

The cost to stay at a campsite is given by the formula:

$C = 10t + 5a + 2c$, where C is the cost in pounds, t is the number of tents, a is the number of adults and c is the number of children.

How much would it cost for 2 adults and 3 children to stay in 1 tent?

$t = 1$, $a = 2$ and $c = 3$, so put these into the formula to find C:
$C = 10 \times 1 + 5 \times 2 + 2 \times 3 = 10 + 10 + 6 = \textbf{£26}$

Remember BODMAS — do the × before the +.

Visualisation Problems

These questions might be similar to some Non-Verbal Reasoning questions, like the ones on pages 15-16.

Visualisation problems are harder <u>shape</u> questions. A shape might be <u>flipped</u> or <u>rotated</u>, and you'll have to <u>picture</u> what it looks like <u>in your head</u>. If you find these questions difficult, try <u>drawing</u> or <u>cutting out</u> the shapes when you're practising.

Example

Shape 1 is made out of square tiles. Thomas makes an identical shape, then rotates it 90° clockwise. He fits this shape together with shape 1 to form shape 2, without any more rotating or flipping.

Which of the shapes below cannot be shape 2?

Shape 1

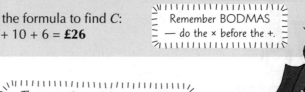

Watch out: you're looking for the one that <u>can't</u> be shape 2.

A   B   C   D   Ⓔ

The answer is **E** — the second shape has been rotated anticlockwise.

Maths

Mixed Topic Problems

You'll probably come across some questions that cover more than one area of Maths. Try to break down the problem into steps that you can solve one at a time.

Example

The bar chart on the right shows the ages of the children in a choir.

Write the ratio of the number of 10-year-olds to the number of 8-year-olds in its simplest form.

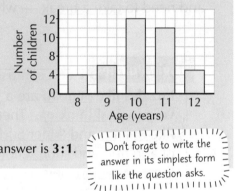

This question is testing bar charts and ratios.
Reading from the chart, the number of 10-year-olds is 12 and the number of 8-year-olds is 4, so the ratio is 12:4.
This can be simplified by dividing both sides by 4 — the answer is **3:1**.

Don't forget to write the answer in its simplest form like the question asks.

Here's another mixed topic question for you to try. The answer is on page 63.

A rectangular room has a width of *w* metres, and is 2 metres longer than it is wide.

Q   What is the correct expression for the area of the room in square metres?

A $w + 2$ **B** $2w + 2$ **C** $2w$ **D** w^2 **E** $(w + 2) \times w$

Don't be put off by algebra sneaking into other questions — the *w* just stands for a number you don't know.

Useful Tips for Tricky Maths Questions

1) Read through the question a couple of times so you know what it's asking.
2) Work out what you know — underline or circle any important details.
3) Work out what you need to do — there might be multiple steps involved.
4) Work out the answer, then check that it looks sensible. Don't forget the units.

Now I'm visualising a world without algebra — so beautiful...

The nice thing about the Maths part of the 11+ is that you should have already learned a lot of this stuff in school. The not-so-nice thing is that there's bound to be a couple of things you haven't covered yet. If you're stuck on a practice question, the best thing to do is to ask for help.

Fun Ways to Prepare for Maths

After a while, you'll probably get tired of just answering lots of maths questions.
Here are a few ways you can improve your maths skills and have fun at the same time.

There are **Fun Ways** to **Practise Maths**

Whether you're preparing for the <u>11+</u> or <u>any other</u> maths test, <u>practice</u> makes <u>perfect</u>.
But there'll come a time when you've <u>had enough</u> of long division and regular polygons
and need to <u>take a break</u> — when that happens, why not try...

Logic Puzzles

Puzzles like <u>Sudoku</u> are a great way to improve
your <u>logical thinking</u>. There are also puzzles
like <u>Kakuro</u> and '<u>killer Sudoku</u>' that involve lots
of <u>addition</u> and <u>subtraction</u>. You can often find
these in <u>newspapers</u>, <u>online</u> or on <u>apps</u>.

1	2	3	9	5	7	8	4	6
4	5	6	2		3	9	1	
7	8	9	4	6	1	3	5	2
	3	2	8	7			9	1
9		1	6		2	7	8	
5	7	8	1	9		2	6	3
3	9	5	7		6	1	2	8
8		7	5	2	9	6	3	
2	6	4		1	8	5	7	9

Every number from 1 to 9 should appear
in every row, column and 3 × 3 square.
Can you work out what number should
go in the shaded square?

Cooking and Baking

This is my <u>favourite</u> one — and not just because you end up with <u>tasty food</u> at
the end of it. Get an adult to let you help with <u>cooking</u> or <u>baking</u> using a <u>recipe</u>.
Tell them that:

- <u>weighing</u> out the ingredients using a set of scales
  is useful practice for <u>measures</u> questions.

- <u>adapting a recipe</u> can improve your <u>proportion</u> skills
  — e.g. if the recipe makes 4 portions, work out how
  much of each ingredient you'd need to serve 6 people.

To serve 4:
300 g spaghetti →
200 g tomatoes

To serve 6:
450 g spaghetti
300 g tomatoes

- <u>dividing</u> the food into <u>equal portions</u> at the end is all about <u>fractions</u>.

- <u>licking the spoon</u> is guaranteed to make you <u>smarter</u>.

OK, that last one is made up, but they don't need to know that...

Fun Ways to Prepare for Maths

Psychic Psusan's Magic Maths

Think of a number — any number.
Now follow these steps:
1. Add 3 to the number.
2. Multiply the result by 4.
3. Next, take away 8.
4. Halve what you've got left.
5. Add on an extra 2.
6. Now halve it again.
7. Finally, take away the number you first thought of.

Using my psychic powers,
I predict that you're left with... 2!

Magic Maths Tricks

Have a go at the 'magic trick' on the left. Then try again with a different number. See if you can figure out how it works (hint: try using algebra). Then have a go at coming up with your own version of the trick. Use it to astound and mystify your friends!

If you like this, there are loads more similar 'tricks' you can find online. Soon all your friends will think you're a mathematical wizard (and they'll be right).

Shopping

Next time you're buying something in a shop, or eating at a restaurant with friends or family, try to work out the total cost in advance. Do a bit of estimating to get a rough idea of the total, then try to figure out the exact amount.

For an extra challenge, figure out how much change you should get when you pay.

Times Tables Challenges

If you've got a competitive streak, why not challenge your friends to a high-speed maths battle? Find an online times tables quiz and race against your friends to see who's the fastest. A dramatic soundtrack is optional, but highly recommended.

Check out CGP's free online
times table tester:
cgpbooks.co.uk/info/times-table-tester

T × 4
Times Tables Time Trials

8 × 6

My high score for the 7 times tables is 35 seconds — see if you can beat it!

No, eating 80% of your birthday cake won't improve your maths...

It's important to have a bit of fun now and then, but there's no substitute for sitting down and doing some questions. Try to strike a balance between serious practice and the fun stuff.

English

The GL test covers English and Verbal Reasoning separately. However, in the CEM test, some of the GL English topics are covered in the Verbal Reasoning section.

There are **Three Main Question Types**

11+ English tests skills like <u>reading</u>, <u>writing</u>, <u>punctuation</u>, <u>spelling</u> and <u>grammar</u>. These are all skills that you'll learn at school, but they might be tested in <u>different</u> or <u>trickier</u> ways in the 11+ assessments.

Here are the <u>three main topics</u> in GL English:

Comprehension

In the test, you'll be given <u>one long text</u> or <u>several shorter texts</u>, followed by some <u>questions</u> about what you've read.

There are <u>three main types</u> of comprehension question:

- <u>Understanding the text</u> — these might ask about things like <u>what happens</u> in the text, the <u>characters</u> and what the writer's <u>purpose</u> is.
- <u>Word meaning</u> — these test your understanding of the <u>vocabulary</u> used in the text.
- <u>Word types and techniques</u> — these test how well you know <u>parts of speech</u> (like nouns or verbs) and <u>literary techniques</u> (like metaphors).

Spelling, Punctuation and Grammar

You'll be given sentences or passages of text and asked to:

- find (and sometimes correct) <u>spelling</u> and <u>punctuation mistakes</u>.
- <u>complete sentences</u> so that they're <u>grammatically correct</u>.

Writing

1) <u>Some tests</u> include a writing task. You'll need to <u>check</u> if your test has one — ask a grown-up if you're not sure.

2) Writing tasks usually last <u>between 20 minutes and an hour</u>. You might have to plan and write a <u>short story</u> or an <u>essay</u>, based on a prompt. You could also be asked to <u>continue</u> the <u>extract</u> from a comprehension question.

English

You Can Also be Asked **Other Types** of Question

There are some <u>other question types</u> that you may come across too.
For example, you could be asked to:

- put words together to make <u>compound words</u>,
  e.g. 'book' and 'shelf' join together to form 'bookshelf'.
- find the <u>odd one out</u> in a list of words.
- <u>reorder words</u> to make a sentence.
- <u>reorder sentences</u> to make a story.

Writing Questions

Here's an example of a <u>GL Writing</u> question:

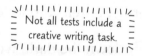
Not all tests include a creative writing task.

Example

Write a story with the title 'The most extraordinary place'.

<u>Plan</u>:
- <u>Beginning</u>
  Iona wakes up in the night, strange glow in garden
- <u>Middle</u>
  Investigates glow — secret door to another world
  Strange world — Iona gets lost, falls in hole
  Found and helped by boy — tells her about the strange world
- <u>End</u>
  Iona's brother appears — followed her in to rescue her

Jot down your plan in note form to save time.

For questions like this, you'll need to:

1) <u>Plan</u> the <u>beginning</u>, <u>middle</u> and <u>end</u> of your story,
   and <u>stick to the plan</u> while you're writing.

2) Write in <u>standard English</u>. Don't use any slang.

3) Use lots of <u>techniques</u>, like similes and
   alliteration, to make your writing <u>interesting</u>.

There are many possible stories you could come up with — this is just an example plan.

English

Whichever test you're taking, you'll need to have a good grasp of spelling and grammar.

Spelling, Punctuation and Grammar Questions

GL English tests spelling, punctuation and grammar separately.

CEM Verbal Reasoning tests your spelling and grammar skills as part of other questions, so make sure you're happy with the basics.

Here is an example of a Spelling question for the GL test:

Example

This passage contains some spelling mistakes.
Each numbered line has either one mistake or no mistakes.
For each line, work out which group of words contains a mistake,
and circle the correct letter. Circle N if there is no mistake.

① **He crept slowly down the dark, winding alleyway, desparate not to make**

| A | B | C | D | N |

② **a sound. The dragon lay sleeping peacefuly at the end of the dungeon.**

| A | B | C | D | N |

③ **Suddenly, its nostrils flared, and a defeaning snore echoed through the castle.**

| A | B | C | D | N |

Answers:
1) **D.** 'desparate' should be 'desperate'.
2) **C.** 'peacefuly' should be 'peacefully' —
   the suffix 'ly' is added to the word 'peaceful'.
3) **C.** 'defeaning' should be 'deafening' — the root word is 'deafen'.

Check each spelling carefully...

Some spelling mistakes might be quite tricky to spot if you don't know the word. Rule out any words you know are correct first, then have a think about the different spelling rules for the rest.

English

Spelling, Punctuation and Grammar Questions

Here is an example of a <u>Punctuation</u> question for the <u>GL test</u>:

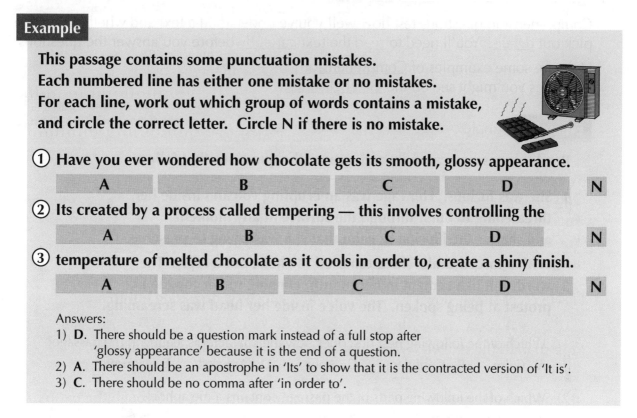

Example

This passage contains some punctuation mistakes.
Each numbered line has either one mistake or no mistakes.
For each line, work out which group of words contains a mistake,
and circle the correct letter. Circle N if there is no mistake.

① Have you ever wondered how chocolate gets its smooth, glossy appearance.

| A | B | C | D | N |

② Its created by a process called tempering — this involves controlling the

| A | B | C | D | N |

③ temperature of melted chocolate as it cools in order to, create a shiny finish.

| A | B | C | D | N |

Answers:
1) **D.** There should be a question mark instead of a full stop after
'glossy appearance' because it is the end of a question.
2) **A.** There should be an apostrophe in 'Its' to show that it is the contracted version of 'It is'.
3) **C.** There should be no comma after 'in order to'.

Here are some things to <u>look out for</u> when you're doing <u>spelling</u>,
<u>punctuation</u> and <u>grammar</u> questions. There are <u>plenty more</u> though
— have a think about everything you've <u>learnt in school</u> too:

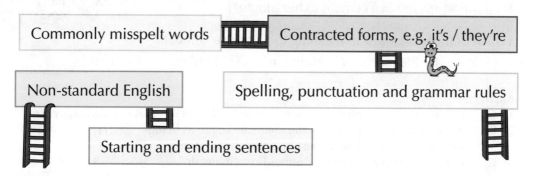

Commonly misspelt words

Contracted forms, e.g. it's / they're

Non-standard English

Spelling, punctuation and grammar rules

Starting and ending sentences

English and Verbal Reasoning

Comprehension is tested in both GL English and CEM Verbal Reasoning.

Comprehension Questions

Comprehension questions test how well you've <u>understood</u> a text and whether you can pick out <u>details</u>. You'll need to <u>read</u> the text <u>carefully</u> before you answer the questions.

Here are some examples of <u>Comprehension</u> questions you might see on the <u>GL English test</u>:

You might see similar questions to some of these in the CEM VR test.

Examples

Read this passage carefully and answer the questions that follow.

1   She was furious. Her rage was an erupting volcano inside her,
    threatening to burst through the surface at any moment
    and shatter the illusion of calm that she was trying to preserve.
    With a forced smile, she attempted to choke out a reply. The
5   words felt like cement in her mouth, clinging to her tongue in
    protest at being spoken. The voice inside her head was screaming.

1) Which of the following best describes how the character is feeling in the passage?
    A Calm   **B** Confident   **C** Angry   **D** Amused   **E** Mournful

2) Which of the following parts of the passage contains a metaphor?
    A   "She was furious"
    B   "Her rage was an erupting volcano inside her"
    C   "With a forced smile"
    D   "she attempted to choke out a reply"
    E   "The words felt like cement in her mouth"

3) Which of these is closest in meaning to "preserve" (line 3)?
    A Safe   **B** Pretend   **C** Maintain   **D** Destroy   **E** Create

Answers:
1) **C**. Line 1 states that the character "was furious". This means that she was angry.
2) **B**. This phrase on line 1 describes the character's rage as being "an erupting volcano", so it must be a metaphor. *Be careful — option E is an example of a simile, not a metaphor.*
3) **C**. "preserve" means the same as "uphold" or "maintain".

English and Verbal Reasoning

Comprehension Questions **Can Vary**

1) There are lots of <u>different types of comprehension text</u> that could come up on your 11+ test, for example:

NON-FICTION
Autobiographies
Informative texts
Instructions
Letters

FICTION
Extracts from novels
Short stories
Myths
Poems

Fiction texts come from the author's imagination. Non-fiction texts are based on facts.

2) Whatever type of text you're given, when <u>answering questions</u> you might find it <u>helpful</u> to:

<u>Highlight or underline key words</u> or <u>phrases</u> as you read the text — ask yourself <u>what</u>, <u>who</u>, <u>why</u>, <u>when</u>, <u>where</u> and <u>how</u>.

<u>Make notes</u> next to the text (in pencil) — if you spot a <u>technique</u> you might be tested on, <u>flag it</u> up.

<u>Highlight</u> key words in the <u>questions</u>. This will help you locate the answer in the <u>parts</u> of the <u>text</u> you've <u>highlighted</u> — e.g. if the question asks '<u>When</u>', you know to look for a <u>time</u> or <u>date</u>.

3) As well as the main question types described on page 28, there are some <u>other</u> types of question that you might come across. Here are some <u>examples</u>:

- <u>Fact recall</u> questions that ask you to find <u>information</u> directly from the passage.
- <u>Reasoning</u> questions that ask you to <u>use clues</u> in the text to <u>work out</u> the answer.
- <u>Multiple-statement</u> questions that ask you to <u>work out</u> which of the statements in a list is <u>true</u> or <u>not true</u>.

GL and CEM comprehension questions are pretty similar...

The main differences between GL and CEM comprehension questions are that there are 5 multiple-choice options for GL but 4 for CEM, and that CEM doesn't ask about word types and techniques.

Verbal Reasoning

Verbal Reasoning might be a completely new subject to you, and that's okay. This page explains what it's all about and then the rest of the section is full of helpful examples.

Verbal Reasoning is **Tested** in **Different Ways**

Verbal Reasoning (VR) is <u>tested differently</u> in different 11+ tests. For example, <u>CEM</u> and <u>GL</u> both ask questions about <u>words</u>, but the <u>GL</u> VR test also includes questions about <u>numbers</u>.

Verbal Reasoning Can be Split into **Topics**

Here are the <u>most common</u> Verbal Reasoning topics for <u>each test</u>:

Comprehension, spelling and grammar are tested in a separate English paper for the GL test (see pages 28-33).

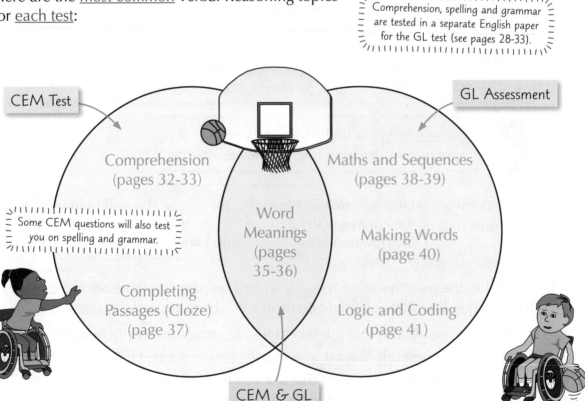

CEM Test

GL Assessment

Comprehension (pages 32-33)

Maths and Sequences (pages 38-39)

Some CEM questions will also test you on spelling and grammar.

Word Meanings (pages 35-36)

Making Words (page 40)

Completing Passages (Cloze) (page 37)

Logic and Coding (page 41)

CEM & GL

Ask an adult to <u>check which topics</u> you'll need to learn for <u>your test</u>.

Verbal Reasoning

Word Meaning questions are covered in both the CEM and the GL tests.

Word Meaning Questions Test Your Vocabulary

1) <u>Word Meaning questions</u> test things such as:

- your <u>understanding</u> of what words mean.
- whether you can <u>compare</u> words.
- whether you can spot <u>similarities</u> and <u>differences</u> in word meanings.
- whether you can see how words are <u>linked</u>.

2) There are <u>different types</u> of Word Meaning question that come up in the CEM and the GL tests:

3) The <u>format</u> of these question types might look <u>different</u> in each type of test.

> Multiple Meanings
> Odd Ones Out
> Closest Meanings — Synonyms
> Opposite Meanings — Antonyms
> Word Connections (GL only)
> Reorder Words to Make a Sentence

Here's an example of a <u>Multiple Meanings</u> question:

Example

Circle the word which has a similar meaning to the words in both sets of brackets.

(agreement   pact)   (decrease   shrink)

  (contract)   promise   dwindle   concur

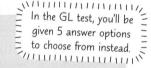
In the GL test, you'll be given 5 answer options to choose from instead.

The answer is '**contract**'. 'contract' can mean 'a deal or arrangement' or 'to become smaller'.

Remember:

- <u>read</u> the <u>question</u> and all of the <u>words</u> carefully before you choose an answer.
- the word you choose has to fit <u>both sets of brackets</u> — some of the answer options might fit for one set but not the other.

Verbal Reasoning

Word Meaning Questions

Here are <u>two types</u> of <u>Closest Meaning</u> (synonym) question — you might see either layout in the CEM test:

> A synonym is a word that means the same as another word. An antonym is a word that means the opposite.

Examples

1) Find a word that means the same, or nearly the same, as the word on the left.

revolting   appealing   (foul)   smoulder   twinkle

The answer is '**foul**'. Both words mean 'disgusting'.

2) Complete the word on the right so that it means the same, or nearly the same, as the word on the left.

revolting   [f] [o] [u] [l]   ← You have to write the missing letters in the boxes.

To <u>help you answer</u> these questions:

- think about the <u>different meanings</u> of the word on the left.
- <u>don't get caught out</u> by antonyms in the answer options — in the example above you need to find the word with the <u>closest meaning</u>, not the <u>opposite meaning</u>.
- <u>read</u> all the options <u>carefully</u> to make sure you've found the word with the <u>closest meaning</u>.
- think about the <u>word type</u> (e.g. noun, verb) of the word on the left — this might help you <u>rule out incorrect</u> answers.

Rule out wrong answers to start with...

When you rule out answer options, you might want to put a light pencil line through them. That way, you won't be distracted by the words that definitely aren't the correct answer.

Verbal Reasoning

This page is specific to the CEM test — if you're taking the GL test, or you know your test won't include Cloze questions, then you can turn the page and be on your way...

Cloze Questions

The CEM test has a type of question called Cloze — this just means that you have to fill in the missing letters or words in a piece of text. Here's an example of a Fill in the Missing Letters question:

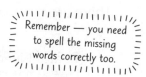

Remember — you need to spell the missing words correctly too.

Example

Fill in the missing letters to complete the words in the following passage:

① **Alex Honnold is a** ☐ a ☐ ☐ u ☐ **rock climber from America.**

② **He began climbing as a child, and** p ☐ r t ☐ c u ☐ ☐ r l y

enjoyed climbing outdoors. In 2017, he became the first person to

③ ☐ s c ☐ ☐ d **the 914-metre-tall landmark 'El Capitan' in Yosemite**

④ **National Park** w ☐ ☐ h o ☐ t **using ropes.**

Answers:
1) **famous** — 'Alex Honnold is a **famous** rock climber'.
2) **particularly** — '**particularly** enjoyed climbing outdoors'.
3) **ascend** — 'to **ascend** the 914-metre-tall landmark'.
4) **without** — '**without** using ropes'.

Make sure the word you've chosen makes sense in the sentence — there may be multiple words that fit but only one that will complete the sentence sensibly.

Alex likes mountains, but I prefer pyramids, so here's a helpful pyramid of things to think about to make sure you spell words correctly.

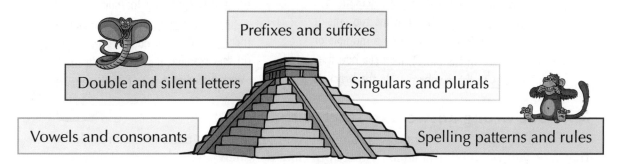

Prefixes and suffixes

Double and silent letters

Singulars and plurals

Vowels and consonants

Spelling patterns and rules

Verbal Reasoning

The next four pages are for the Verbal Reasoning section of the GL test — if you're taking the CEM test, or know they aren't relevant to your test, then head to page 42.

Maths and Sequences Questions

There are <u>five</u> main Maths and Sequences <u>question types</u> to look out for:

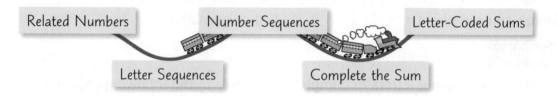

Related Numbers   Number Sequences   Letter-Coded Sums

Letter Sequences   Complete the Sum

Some of these question types involve <u>numbers</u> — so you'll need to be confident with <u>basic maths skills</u>, like <u>addition</u>, <u>subtraction</u>, <u>division</u> and <u>multiplication</u>. Make sure you know your <u>times tables</u> and are comfortable doing <u>mental maths</u>.

Here's an example of a <u>Related Numbers</u> question:

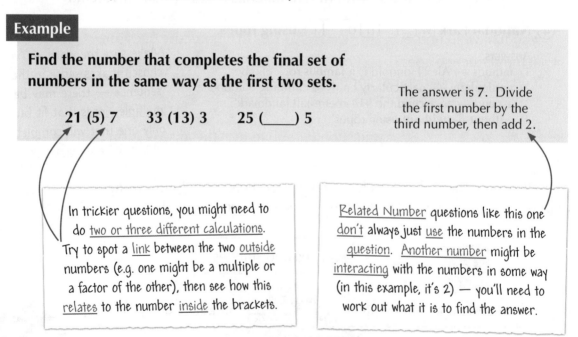

Example

Find the number that completes the final set of numbers in the same way as the first two sets.

21 (5) 7   33 (13) 3   25 (____) 5

The answer is **7**. Divide the first number by the third number, then add 2.

In trickier questions, you might need to do <u>two or three different calculations</u>. Try to spot a <u>link</u> between the two <u>outside</u> numbers (e.g. one might be a multiple or a factor of the other), then see how this <u>relates</u> to the number <u>inside</u> the brackets.

<u>Related Number</u> questions like this one <u>don't</u> always just <u>use</u> the numbers in the question. <u>Another number</u> might be interacting with the numbers in some way (in this example, it's 2) — you'll need to work out what it is to find the answer.

Verbal Reasoning

Maths and Sequences Questions

In questions about <u>sequences</u>, you'll need to <u>spot</u> and <u>continue patterns</u> in sequences of <u>letters</u> and <u>numbers</u>.

Here's an example of a <u>Letter Sequences</u> question:

Example

Find the pair of letters that continues the sequence in the best way. Use the alphabet to help you.

A B C D E F G H I J K L M N O P Q R S T U V W X Y Z

LT	**JU**	**HW**	**FZ**	**DD**
A CI	**B** BI	**C** AI	**D** BH	**E** CH

The answer is **B**. The first letter moves back two letters at a time. The second letter moves in the sequence +1, +2, +3, +4, +5.

- If the <u>first</u> and <u>second letters</u> in each pair follow <u>different patterns</u>, you'll have to find <u>two different sequences</u> to answer the question.
- If the sequence goes <u>past Z</u> or <u>before A</u>, just <u>loop</u> to the other end of the alphabet and continue in the <u>same direction</u>. —

Here is a <u>Letter-Coded Sums</u> question for you to try. The answer is on page 63.

Each letter stands for a number.
Work out the answer to the sum as a letter.

 A = 3   B = 4   C = 7   D = 12   E = 24

B × A + D = (_____)

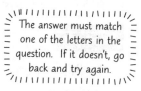

The answer must match one of the letters in the question. If it doesn't, go back and try again.

Jot down each step in the sequence as you go...

It's a good idea to write down your working for Maths and Sequences questions — you might need to think about a few numbers or letters at once, so it'll stop you getting confused.

Verbal Reasoning

Making Words Questions

There are different types of Making Words questions:

These ask you to form new words — for example, by finding missing letters, or by spotting the pattern that was used to make a word.

You'll need your spelling and eye-for-patterns hats on for these ones.

> Missing Letters
> Move a Letter
> Hidden Word
> Find the Missing Word
> Use a Rule to Make a Word
> Compound Words
> Complete a Word Pair
> Anagrams in a Sentence

Here's an example of a Missing Letters question:

Example

Find the letter that will finish the first word and start the second word of each pair. The same letter must be used for both pairs.

> **cas (?) ick   duc (?) now**
>
> **A** t   **B** h   **©** k   **D** c   **E** l

The answer is **C**. The letter 'k' can be used to make the words 'cask', 'kick', 'duck' and 'know'.

- Use the options to help you — try each one until you find the correct answer.
- Make sure the letter works for all four of the words — i.e. 't' would work for the first three in this example, but not the last one.

Here's an example of a Hidden Word question:

Example

In the sentence below, a four-letter word is hidden at the end of one word and the start of the next. Find the part of the sentence that contains the hidden word.

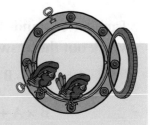

> **He saw two red robins outside.**
>
> **A** He saw   **B** saw two   **©** two red   **D** red robins   **E** robins outside

The answer is **C**, 'two red'. The hidden word is 'wore'.

Verbal Reasoning

Logic and Coding Questions

Logic and coding is all about <u>interpreting information</u>.
These are the <u>main question types</u> you might see:

Letter Connections
Letter-Word Codes
Number-Word Codes
Explore the Facts
Solve the Riddle

Here is an example of a <u>Solve the Riddle</u> question:

Example

Read the information carefully, then use it to answer the question that follows.

A group of friends went to a school disco together. Jonny danced to two songs with Sara. Sara also danced with Maylin. Freddie danced with Amir. Maylin only danced with two people. Amir danced with all of the friends. Nobody danced with anyone else.

If the statements above are true, only one of the sentences below cannot be true. Which one?

A Jonny and Maylin danced with the same people.

B Amir was the only person who danced with Freddie.

C Freddie is a really good dancer.

(D) Sara danced with the most people.

E Jonny danced with Sara the most.

The answer is **D**. Sara danced with three people — Jonny, Maylin and Amir. Amir danced with four people, as he danced with everyone. Therefore, Sara cannot have danced with the most people.

Here are some <u>tips</u> for when you're doing questions like this:

- <u>Make notes</u> about how the information links together — this will help you work out <u>which</u> of the statements <u>cannot be true</u>.

- Some <u>answer options</u> (like C in the example above) <u>won't be mentioned</u> in the statements — you <u>won't be able to prove</u> that they're <u>not true</u>, so you can <u>rule them out</u>.

> Make sure you only make notes in pencil and on spare paper, not the test paper.

Fun Ways to Prepare for English & VR

You can prepare for the 11+ in lots of ways. It's important to do practice questions, but it's also a good idea to mix your practice up to avoid getting bored or losing focus.

Focus on Improving Your **Vocabulary** and **Writing** Skills

You can do lots in your <u>day-to-day life</u> that will help you with your <u>11+ preparation</u> — here are some suggestions:

WRITE STORIES

<u>Creative writing</u> helps you develop your <u>communication</u> and <u>writing</u> skills, as well as letting you use your <u>imagination</u> in a really fun way.

READ

Reading is the perfect way to <u>improve</u> your <u>vocabulary</u> and <u>understanding</u> of texts — both <u>fiction</u> and <u>non-fiction</u>. Go on, lose yourself in a good book (headstand encouraged, but optional).

SOLVE ANAGRAMS

Ask someone to <u>jumble words up</u> for you (or you might even find <u>lists</u> of anagrams on the <u>internet</u>), then <u>time yourself</u> to see how quickly you can <u>solve</u> them.

WRITE ARTICLES

Try writing short <u>newspaper</u> or <u>magazine</u> articles about things that happen during your day — get <u>creative</u>!

WRITE LETTERS

Letter-writing (to friends, relatives or pen-pals) will help you practise your <u>spelling</u>, <u>grammar</u>, <u>punctuation</u> and <u>formal writing</u> skills.

KEEP A DIARY

Writing a diary entry every day is a great way to practise your <u>writing skills</u> and use some of the <u>new vocab</u> you've learnt.

Fun Ways to Prepare for English & VR

Make the Most of Newspapers and Magazines

Pick a short article to read each day and underline any words you don't know. Look up their definitions in a dictionary and write them down in a notepad. At the end of the week, look over the list and see how many you can remember. You'll be surprised by how many will stick!

Summarise Your Way to Success

Picking out key facts from a text is an important skill for comprehension questions. Before you get rid of the articles you read, have a go at summarising them to an adult — keep it to three or four sentences if you can. If they're busy, you could try telling the cat, but you might not get much of a response...

Word Puzzles

Another fun way to develop your 11+ skills is to do puzzles like word searches, crosswords and codewords. Word puzzles will increase your vocabulary, help your problem-solving skills and get you used to seeing incomplete words — all essential skills for 11+ success!

A little goes a long way...

These additions to your daily routine only take up a small amount of time, but they could make a big difference when it comes to developing key skills for the 11+.

Fun Ways to Prepare for English & VR

You know the famous expression, "variety is the spice of 11+ preparation"...

Activities and Games Can Make 11+ Practice Fun

Twenty Questions and CLUEDO

Games like Twenty Questions and CLUEDO help you develop your logic and reasoning skills. Remembering information and working your way through facts will come in really useful for your 11+ preparation.

Playing board games like SCRABBLE ® and BANANAGRAMS ®, where you have to form words from a set of letters, is a great way of increasing your vocabulary and practising spelling. Plus, you'll be much quicker at solving anagrams!

Flashcards

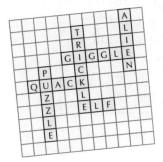

Vocabulary flashcards are small cards with a word on one side and its definition on the other side. They're really handy for learning words that you're finding hard to remember — and because they're pocket-sized, you can test yourself on the go!

You can find these on the internet, or you could make your own — writing the words for yourself will help you learn them.

Before the Test

You've practised and practised, and now test day is nearly here.
Here are a few things to do to make sure you're in tip-top condition and ready to go.

Do Final Preparations the **Night Before**

Spend time the night before the test making sure you're prepared:

1) Get anything you're taking into the test ready to go.

2) Make sure you know what time you're leaving.

3) Do something relaxing or some gentle exercise.

4) Try to get a good night's sleep.

Test Kit Checklist

- A few HB pencils ☑
- A rubber ☑
- A pencil sharpener ☑
- A watch ☑

Wake Up at a **Sensible Time**

Discuss with your parents or carers what time you should wake up. Agree whether you'll set an alarm or if they'll wake you up.

Have a good breakfast — you don't want to get hungry.

Don't try to learn anything new — save your energy for the test.

> If you've practised doing tests first thing in the morning, you'll be ready to go on test day.

Arrive at Your Test in **Plenty of Time**

When you get to the test venue, find out where you need to wait.

Make sure you get there early so that you have time to relax before the test starts. Try not to arrive at the test too early — you don't want a long wait.

Make sure you can hear any instructions — you'll be told where to go for the test and where you need to sit.

Take a deep breath and wiggle your toes...

It's normal to feel a bit nervous before a test — lots of people will be feeling the same way.
Try thinking about something else while you wait — football, your dog, the weather, my dog...

During the Test

Now it's test time. The key here is to focus and not to rush.

Organise Your Desk Space

While you're waiting for the test to start:

Get your <u>pencils,</u> <u>rubber</u> and <u>sharpener</u> out.

Place your <u>watch</u> on your desk.

<u>Listen</u> to any <u>instructions</u> given to you.

Fill in the <u>front</u> of your test paper.

Take some <u>deep breaths</u> to calm yourself.

Focus on What You're Doing During the Test

1) <u>Read</u> each question <u>carefully</u>. Then read each question <u>again</u>.

2) If you're <u>not sure</u> of an answer, make a <u>sensible guess</u>. For tricky multiple-choice questions, try to rule out any options which are <u>definitely wrong</u>. You can then <u>guess</u> from the options that are left.

3) Keep an eye on the <u>time</u>. Any time left at the end can be used to <u>check your answers</u>, or to go back to any questions you've <u>missed out</u>.

4) <u>Don't get distracted</u> by what anyone else is doing.

Dealing with Test Troubles

⭐  If you can't answer a question...
Move on to the next question and come back to it later (if you have time).

⭐ If you're running out of time...
Leave any tricky questions and move on to ones you think you can do.

⭐  If you realise that you've got a question wrong...
Rub out what you've done and clearly mark your new answer.

After the Test

You've done it. You've worked hard, so you should be proud of yourself.

Don't Worry... it's Over!

It's okay to not want to talk about the test with your
friends if you think it will make you worried or upset.

> You'll have to wait a while until you get your results. There's
> nothing more you can do now, so try not to worry about
> your answers — you can't change what you wrote in the test.

Take Some Time Out to Relax

1) Tests are tiring — try to relax after the test or do something fun (see next page).

2) If you're feeling unhappy or anxious, doing some exercise could help.

3) And finally...

BE HAPPY THAT YOU'VE FINISHED THE 11+!

~~Sing and Dance Around~~* Unwind After the Test is Over

1) When the 11+ is over, store your study books and practice papers out of sight.

2) Celebrate your hard work — spend time with friends,
   play some fun games or go on an exciting trip.

Give yourself a high five and a well-earned pat on the back...

Try to put the 11+ to the back of your mind until results day. If you find yourself thinking about
it too much, do something to help take your mind off it, such as writing a song about bananas.

*Well, you can if you want — but wait till you're outside the test hall.

After the Test

After all that hard work, it's time to do something you enjoy to celebrate.
Use this page to plan a fun activity to do when you've finished the 11+.

MY FUN ACTIVITY IS...

When am I going to do it?

Where am I going?

Who else is coming?

What equipment do I need?

What clothes do I need to wear?

Using the Topic Planners

The last part of this book is a <u>Study Planner</u>. It contains <u>Topic Planners</u> and a <u>Study Diary</u> to help <u>organise</u> your 11+ study and preparation, so you're ready when test day arrives.

> Your Topic Planners and Study Diary can be found on pages 51-63 of this book. There are spaces for you to fill them out yourself to help you keep track of your progress.

Break each Subject Down into Topics

There is <u>one</u> Topic Planner for <u>each subject</u>:
Non-Verbal Reasoning, Maths, English and Verbal Reasoning.

Fill in the <u>Topic Planners</u> on pages 51-54 for each subject (see below).
We've <u>started</u> each of them for you, but you'll need to <u>complete</u> them all.

1. Find a <u>list of topics</u> or <u>question types</u> that come up in each subject (you could look in a study book or ask an adult).

2. Put a <u>tick</u> in the <u>column</u> that shows how <u>happy</u> you are with each topic. <u>Update</u> each topic in the table when you feel more <u>confident</u>.

3. Keep practising until you're <u>happy</u> with <u>each topic</u>.

Don't worry if you're unsure about a lot of your topics at first. The whole point of studying and practising is that you get more confident as you go on.

Example:

Non-Verbal Reasoning

Topic	☹	😐	😊
Similarities and Differences	✓		
Odd One Out	✓	✓	
Find the Figure Like the Others	✓		
Complete the Pair	✓		
Complete the Series	✓	✓	
Complete the Grid	✓		

Using the Study Diary

It's useful to keep a <u>Study Diary</u> to record everything you do to prepare for the 11+. It will help you to <u>keep track</u> of <u>what</u> you've done so far, <u>how well</u> it went and what skills you need to <u>improve</u>.

Write in the <u>date</u>. ①

Date	Tuesday 9th July
What I Did	Helped bake a birthday cake for my brother. Converted the masses of all the ingredients ② from grams to kilograms.
How It Went	Got all of the conversions correct and the cake was very tasty too!
What I Need To Do Next	Do some questions to practise converting different units and measures.
Date	Thursday 11th July
What I Did	Maths Algebra Practice Questions
How It Went	Only got 6 out of 15 questions right. ③
What I Need To Do Next	Go back to my study book and read about how to do algebra questions again. Then do some more practice questions. ④

Each time you study, write down <u>what you have done</u>. You can also include any <u>fun activities</u> you've done to help you develop your skills.

Comment on <u>how your studying went</u>. Did you understand what you read? How many questions did you get right?

Write down what you could do next to help <u>develop</u> your 11+ skills and <u>improve</u>.

Topic Planner — Non-Verbal Reasoning

We've started it for you, you lucky thing, but it's over to you to finish it off.

Topic	😕	🙂	😉
Similarities and Differences			
Odd One Out			
Find the Figure Like the Others			

Don't worry if you don't fill in all the rows — just use as many as you need.

Topic Planner — Maths

Topic	😖	🙂	😉
Working with Numbers — Place Value			
Working with Numbers — Rounding			
Working with Numbers — Addition			

Topic Planner — English

You'll only need this page if your 11+ test includes English.

Topic	🙁	😐	😊
Grammar — Nouns and Pronouns			
Grammar — Verbs			
Grammar — Adjectives and Adverbs			

Topic Planner — Verbal Reasoning

Topic	😟	🙂	😉
Word Meanings — Multiple Meanings			
Word Meanings — Odd Ones Out			
Word Meanings — Closest Meanings			

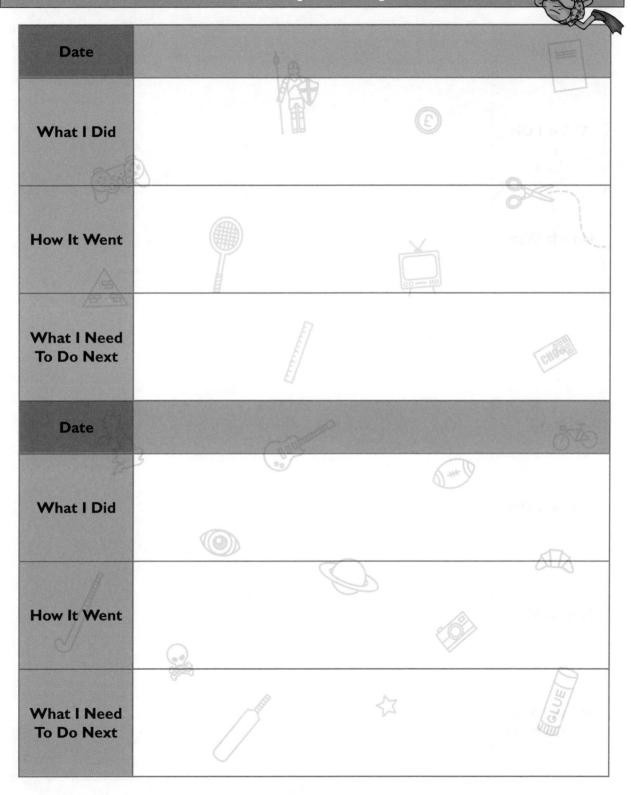

Study Diary

Date	
What I Did	
How It Went	
What I Need To Do Next	
Date	
What I Did	
How It Went	
What I Need To Do Next	

Study Diary

Date	
What I Did	
How It Went	
What I Need To Do Next	
Date	
What I Did	
How It Went	
What I Need To Do Next	

57

Study Diary

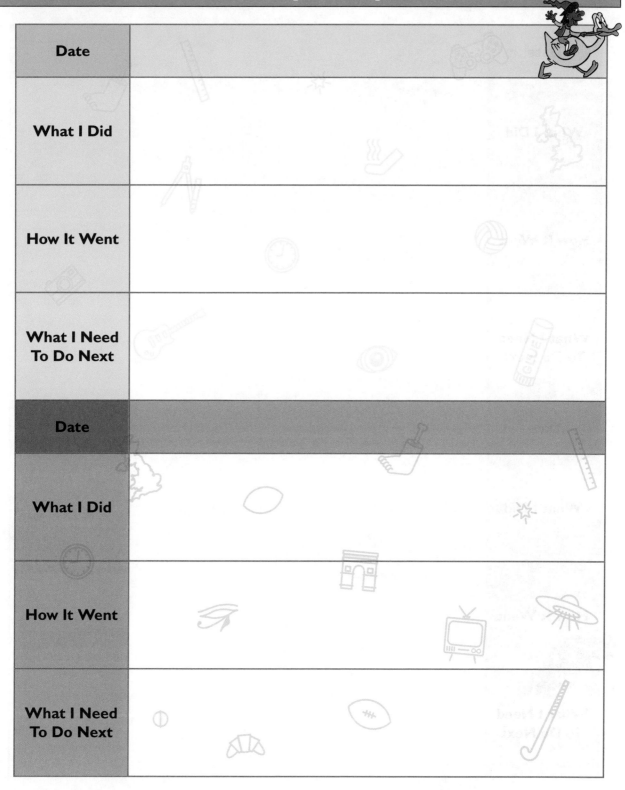

Date	
What I Did	
How It Went	
What I Need To Do Next	
Date	
What I Did	
How It Went	
What I Need To Do Next	

Study Diary

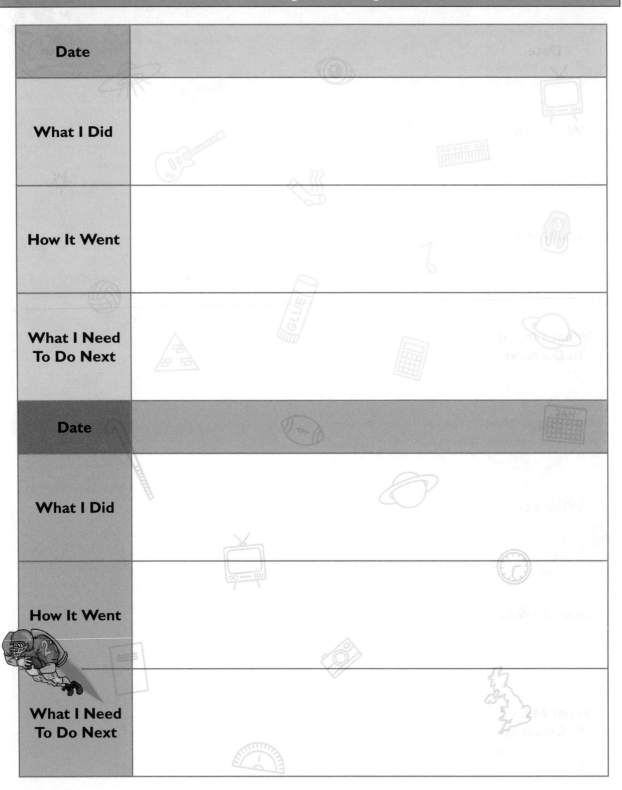

Date	
What I Did	
How It Went	
What I Need To Do Next	
Date	
What I Did	
How It Went	
What I Need To Do Next	

Study Diary

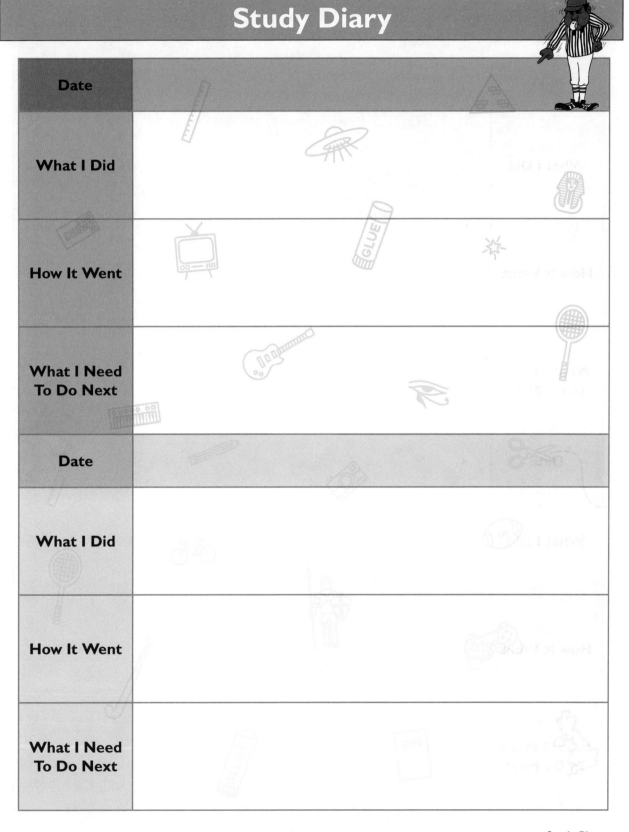

Date	
What I Did	
How It Went	
What I Need To Do Next	
Date	
What I Did	
How It Went	
What I Need To Do Next	

Study Diary

Date	
What I Did	
How It Went	
What I Need To Do Next	
Date	
What I Did	
How It Went	
What I Need To Do Next	

Study Diary

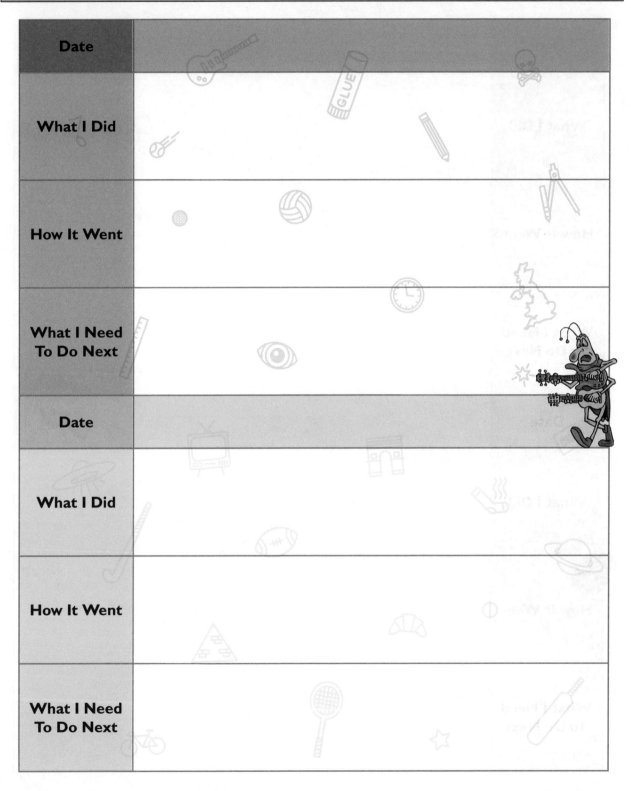

Date	
What I Did	
How It Went	
What I Need To Do Next	
Date	
What I Did	
How It Went	
What I Need To Do Next	

Study Diary

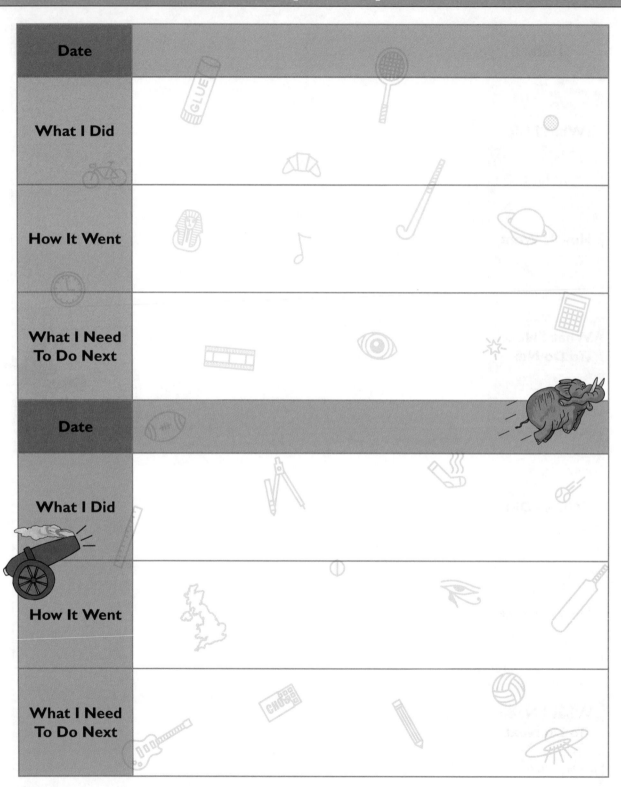

Date	
What I Did	
How It Went	
What I Need To Do Next	
Date	
What I Did	
How It Went	
What I Need To Do Next	

Study Diary

Date	
What I Did	
How It Went	
What I Need To Do Next	

Answers

Page 13 — Similarities and Differences

The answer is **d**.
All figures must have a square, a pentagon and a hexagon. The biggest shape must be white and in front of the other shapes. There must only be one grey shape.

Page 16 — 3D Shapes and Folding

The answer is **e**.
Option **a** is ruled out because if the rectangles are at the front of the cube and the white square is on the right, then the star should be on the top.
Option **b** is ruled out because the net doesn't have two identical faces. Option **c** is ruled out because the star is white instead of grey. Option **d** is ruled out because the cube face with the arrow and the cube face with the white square must be on opposite sides.

Page 21 — Working with Numbers

The answer is **6912**.
54 is double 27, so the answer is double 3456.
$2 \times 3456 = 6912$.

Page 25 — Mixed Topic Problems

The answer is **E**.
To find the area of a rectangle, you multiply the length by the width.
Width = w m, and length = width + 2 m = $w + 2$ m.
So length × width = $(w + 2) \times w$ m².

Page 39 — Maths and Sequences

The answer is **E**.
$4 \times 3 + 12 = 24$, E = 24.

Top Tips for 11+ Success

Here are our super-duper, tip-top, best-of-all-time, can't-be-beaten 11+ preparation tips:

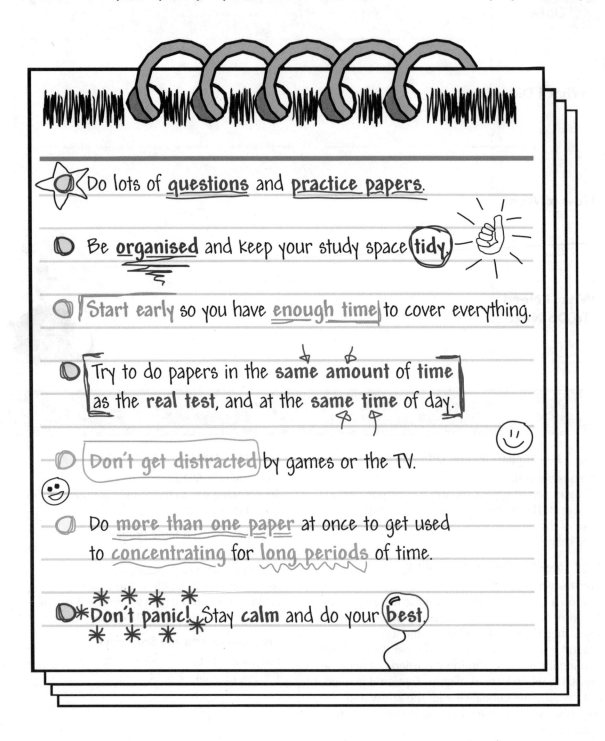

- Do lots of **questions** and **practice papers**.
- Be **organised** and keep your study space tidy.
- Start early so you have **enough time** to cover everything.
- Try to do papers in the **same amount** of time as the **real test**, and at the **same time** of day.
- Don't get distracted by games or the TV.
- Do more than one paper at once to get used to concentrating for long periods of time.
- *Don't panic! Stay **calm** and do your best.*

XHRE1

Study Planner